IMAGES
of America

ROXBURY

Maurice Tobin (1901–1953) and his family pose in the parlor of their Alleghaney Street home on Mission Hill, Roxbury, about 1933. Tobin, for whom the bridge spanning the Mystic River was named, served as state representative from Roxbury, governor of Massachusetts from 1945 to 1947, and United States Secretary of Labor from 1948 to 1952. (Courtesy of the Boston Public Library, hereinafter referred to as the BPL.)

IMAGES
of America

ROXBURY

Anthony Mitchell Sammarco

ARCADIA

First published 1997
Copyright © Anthony Mitchell Sammarco, 1997

ISBN 0-7524-0542-X

Published by Arcadia Publishing,
an imprint of the Chalford Publishing Corporation,
One Washington Center, Dover, New Hampshire 03820.
Printed in Great Britain

Library of Congress Cataloging-in-Publication Data applied for

The 1962 New England Baptist Hospital School of Nursing basketball team was the winner of the Nurses' League title that year. Wearing gym jumpers with "NEBH" in bold letters, they pose for their photograph following their victory. (Courtesy of the New England Baptist Hospital.)

Contents

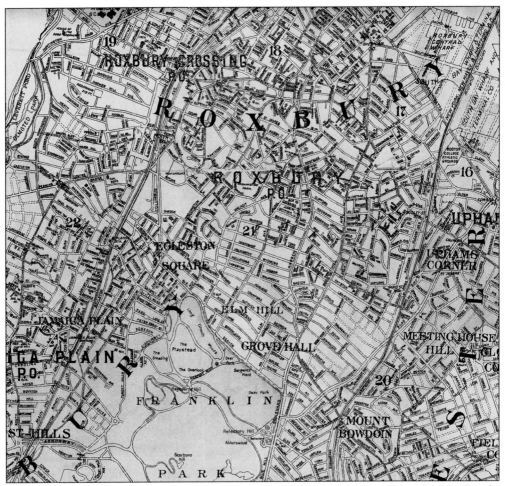

In this 1909 map taken from the *Roxbury Blue Book*, one can see many Roxbury neighborhoods, such as Grove Hall, Elm Hill, Egleston Square, Parker Hill, Mission Hill, and Roxbury Crossing. (Courtesy of Stephen D. Paine.)

Introduction

Roxbury was settled on September 28, 1630, by William Pynchon and a group of fellow Puritans who left England for the New World in pursuit of religious freedom. They settled in what was to become one of the more affluent towns in colonial America, a town that derived its name from the outcroppings and ledges of stone that later became known as "Roxbury Puddingstone." Through the poem *"The Dorchester Giant"* by Oliver Wendell Holmes, the outcroppings of stone that dotted the town were not only satirized, but immortalized as the pudding of the giant's children; obviously they disliked the pudding or were just typical children, for Holmes said in his poem:

> They flung it over the Roxbury hills,
> They flung it over the plain,
> And all over Milton and Dorchester too
> Great lumps of pudding the giants threw;
> They tumbled as thick as rain.
>
> Giant and mammoth have passed away,
> For ages have floated by;
> The suet is hard as a marrowbone,
> And every plum is turned to a stone,
> But there the puddings lie.

Throughout the seventeenth and eighteenth centuries, Roxbury provided the only access by land to Boston via "The Neck." Boston was an 800-acre peninsula that was connected to the mainland at Roxbury. The Roxbury Meetinghouse was at Eliot Square, named for the Reverend John Eliot (1604–1691), who was known as the "Apostle to the Indians." He translated the Bible into the language of the Native Americans and served as "teacher" (minister) in Roxbury until his death. The proximity of the town to Boston led to its use as a place of country estates for Royal Governor William Shirley's "Shirley Place" (now the Shirley-Eustis House) and many other noted members of the colonial elite. Following the Revolution, Roxbury became far more attractive to Bostonians who sought open land for their estates. By 1839, Roxbury was serviced by horse-drawn omnibuses that brought residents to Boston every fifteen minutes from the Norfolk House on Meeting House Hill and had "5 churches in this village, 2 Congregational, 1 Baptist, 1 Episcopal, and 1 Universalist. There are two banks, the 'Peoples' and 'Winthrop,' each with capital of $100,000."

By the mid-nineteenth century, Roxbury was a delightful country town that had "numerous genteel residences and cottages, which are mostly built of wood and painted white, [and] contrast strongly with the evergreens and shrubbery by which most of them are surrounded."

However, Roxbury's proximity to the city of Boston brought great changes to the town, and Roxbury became an independent city in 1846. The greatest change took place in the decade between 1840 and 1850, when "the population increased from nine thousand to eighteen thousand." As a result of this growth, the western section of Roxbury separated from the city in 1851 and incorporated itself as the Town of West Roxbury, which included the present neighborhoods of West Roxbury, Roslindale, and Jamaica Plain. In the period between 1846, the year Roxbury was incorporated as a city, and 1867, the year it was annexed by the City of Boston, Roxbury had become a thriving place that attracted new residents who not only commuted to Boston for business but also worked in the numerous mills, factories, and breweries that were built in the once suburban town.

After Roxbury was annexed to Boston in 1867, the changes became marked; the population soared and the subdivision and development of the farms and estates led to new streets and new houses that seemed to spring up as if by magic. By the turn of the century, Roxbury was a neighborhood of Boston that was served by streetcars from downtown and the Elevated Railway, commonly known as the "El." The Elevated Railway connected Dudley Street in Roxbury to Sullivan Square in Charlestown, and the train stations were designed by Alexander Wadsworth Longfellow (1854–1943). Roxbury was no longer home to just the descendants of the original settlers and the Yankees who created "Boston Highlands," as it was known after the annexation, but was also the home of immigrants from Ireland and Germany who settled in the Mission Hill and Stony Brook Valley and were employed in the factories. Roxbury later became home to many of the German, Polish, and Russian Jews who immigrated to this country during the late nineteenth century and who built their synagogues on the streets that had been laid out by the developers in the mid-nineteenth century. Many of the churches and synagogues were later to be adapted as places of worship and schools by the African-Americans who had begun settling in the neighborhood at the turn of the century after leaving the western slope of Beacon Hill and the South End. With churches and synagogues serving the religious needs of the residents, the diverse and exciting aspects of change could be correlated to a ballet, as described by Theodore White (1915–1986) in his book *In Search of History*. White described the neighborhood in the late nineteenth century as an evolving place where "old stock Protestants gave way to the Irish, who gave way in turn to Italians or Jews, who gave way in turn to blacks." White, the son of Russian Jews, was raised near Grove Hall, the thriving junction of Washington and Warren Streets and Blue Hill and Geneva Avenues. This migration was not unique to Roxbury, or even to Boston, but was a shared experience of every inner city neighborhood along the Eastern Seaboard.

Roxbury has an immensely rich and ever-evolving history. Its early history is known for the accomplishments of Reverend John Eliot and the Roxbury Latin School, the oldest preparatory school in this country. However, the history of Roxbury in the century following its incorporation as a city, from 1846 to 1946, is a fascinating spectrum of American history and development and is extolled in this photographic history. Since the beginning of the town of "Rocksberry" in 1630, a wide variety of ethnic, religious, and racial groups have immigrated and settled in the town, calling it "Home." Roxbury is a thriving nexus of cultures that offers much material for the understanding of what a Boston neighborhood truly represents.

One
Early Roxbury

Meeting House Hill in Roxbury was sketched in 1790 by John Ritto Penniman, an artist and eglomisè painter for the noted clockmaker Simon Willard. The Roxbury Meetinghouse, which had been built in 1746, can be seen in the center with the houses near Eliot Square. During the Revolutionary War, Meeting House Hill was referred to as "Tory Hill," and the common was used as a parade ground where General Washington reviewed the colonial troops.

William Pynchon (1589–1661) a "gentleman of learning and religion," is considered the founder of Roxbury, which was settled in 1630. Pynchon later settled Springfield, Massachusetts, and became known as a difficult Puritan after the publication of his book *The Meritorious Price of Our Redemption*, which was publicly burned! (Courtesy of the West Roxbury Historical Society.)

John Eliot (1604–1690) translated the Bible into the language of the Native Americans. The title page of his translation, *Up-Biblum God naneeswe Nukkone Testament kah Wonk Wusku Testament*, was printed by Samuel Green in 1663.

The Crafts House was built in 1709 by Ebenezer Crafts and stood on Huntington Avenue, opposite Parker Hill. Though considered an "ancient house" and a noted landmark, it was nonetheless demolished in 1900. (Courtesy of the West Roxbury Historical Society.)

The Mead-Munroe House was built in 1683 on Warren Street, near Saint James Street. The farm originally extended from below Tolman Place to Walnut Avenue. It was demolished in 1910.

The First Church of Roxbury was photographed about 1870 from Eliot Square. This was the fifth meetinghouse to be built, and upon its completion in 1804, the church proved an impressive and elegant place of worship. (Courtesy of the BPL.)

The Dillaway-Thomas House was built c. 1750 by Reverend Oliver Peabody as his parsonage. During the Siege of Boston, it was the headquarters of General Thomas, and from its windows could be seen the movement of the British troops, the Battle of Bunker Hill, and the evacuation of Boston. Charles Knapp Dillaway was the headmaster of the Boston Latin School, and here he educated the first Japanese students to journey to this country for an education.

"Shirley Place" was the country estate of William Shirley, governor of Massachusetts Bay. Designed by Peter Harrison, who also designed King's Chapel in Boston, the elegant country seat faces Dudley Street and has a cupola that has provided superb views of the surrounding countryside for over two and a half centuries.

William Shirley (1693–1771) was governor of Massachusetts Bay from 1741 to 1756. Shirley served as commander in chief of the British army in North America in 1755 and lieutenant general in 1759. "Shirley was a man of great industry and ability, but though able, enterprising, and deservedly popular, was ambitious in a degree disproportionate to his powers."

13

Increase Sumner (1746 –1799) was governor of the Commonwealth of Massachusetts from 1797 to his death. He represented Roxbury in the General Court and in the Senate and also served as Associate Justice of the United States Supreme Court.

The Auchmuty House was at the corner of Washington and Cliff Streets and had been built by Judge Robert Auchmuty. The estate was confiscated during the Revolutionary War as the property of a Tory and was subsequently purchased by Governor Increase Sumner. (Courtesy of the West Roxbury Historical Society.)

The Honorable Ebenezer Seaver, for whom Seaver Street was named, was known as the "Squire" and served as a member of the United States House of Representatives. He was a gentleman farmer, and his estate, "The Long Crouch," was where the Seckel pear and the Seaver Sweeting apple were first introduced to this country. (Courtesy of the West Roxbury Historical Society.)

Dr. William Eustis (1753–1825) was governor of the Commonwealth of Massachusetts from 1823 to 1825, as well as a medical doctor who had studied under Dr. Joseph Warren. He purchased Shirley Place in 1819 for his country house and entertained visitors, including LaFayette and Webster, to the most lavish hospitality. It was said of Eustis that his "urbanity, his social qualities, and his hospitality procured him the acquaintance of many persons of distinction."

15

General William Heath (1738–1814), for whom Heath Street was named, was a captain of the Ancient and Honorable Artillery Company and a delegate to the Provincial Congresses of 1774 and 1775. He was commander of West Point and a delegate to the convention that adopted the Constitution of the United States.

Meeting House Hill in Roxbury was sketched in 1839 by John Warner Barber for his book *Historical Collections of Massachusetts*. A horse-drawn omnibus passes the common in front of the First Parish Church, and on the right is the Norfolk House.

NORFOLK HOUSE....ROXBURY.

The old Norfolk House was built as a residence in 1781 by Joseph Ruggles. After his death, it was purchased by David Simmons, who in turn sold it in 1825 to the Norfolk House Company. A large brick addition was built in the rear and was known as Highland Hall, then as Norfolk Hall; the hall was enlarged in 1850.

When the present structure was built, the Norfolk House was moved back to the rear. The hotel, pictured here in 1869, was both impressive and fashionable. The H.S. Lawrence & Company Clothing Store was on the first floor; the Roxbury Neighborhood House and a branch of the library were also located here for many years.

The Lambert House was built on Bartlett Street just after the Revolutionary War. It later became the Ladies' Unity Club Home for Aged People. (Courtesy of William F. Clark.)

In 1800, Captain Stoddard built Ionic Hall as a home for his daughter, Mrs. Hammond. Located on Roxbury Street, across from the Roxbury Meetinghouse, the building was later to become Saint Luke's Home for Convalescents. Today, it is part of the Roxbury Heritage Park.

Edward Everett Hale (1822–1909) lived in an impressive Greek Revival mansion at 39 Highland Street. Author of *A Man Without A Country*, Hale was a respected clergyman, serving as pastor of the South Congregational Church in Boston. His book *Ten Times One is Ten* led to the establishment of clubs devoted to charity, which became prolific throughout the country. The house was later moved to 12 Morley Street in 1914, when it was converted to apartments.

At the junction of Warren Street and Walnut Avenue stood Highland Hall, built about 1850 completely out of Roxbury puddingstone. (Courtesy of William F. Clark.)

The old Warren House was built in 1720 on Warren Street and was sketched in 1852 for Frederick Gleason's *Pictorial Drawing Room Companion*. The Warren family was among the most prominent of Roxbury families, and Warren Square, just opposite the house, was named in memory of Joseph Warren, who was born in this house.

General Joseph Warren (1741–1775) was born in Roxbury and attended Roxbury Latin School and Harvard College. He was a medical doctor, orator, and patriot who died during the Battle of Bunker Hill on June 17, 1775. (Courtesy of the Gibson House Museum.)

Dr. John Warren (1753–1815) was the brother of Joseph Warren and an eminent physician and anatomist. Dr. Warren was Professor of Anatomy and Surgery at Harvard for twenty-three years and was "the first surgeon of his time in New England, if not in the United States."

The Warren family demolished the old Warren House and built a stone cottage on its site in 1846 dedicated to the memory of Joseph and John Warren. Known as the "Warrenhurst," a tablet on the house states, "On this spot stood the house erected in 1720 by Joseph Warren of Boston, remarkable for being the birthplace of Gen. Joseph Warren, his grandson who was killed at the battle of Bunker Hill, June 17, 1775." Two boys lean against the stone wall in this turn-of-the-century photograph.

A monument to Joseph Warren was erected in 1904 at Warren Square, the junction of Warren, Moreland, Regent, Saint James, and Cliff Streets. Sculpted in Paris by Paul Wayland Bartlett (1865–1925), it had the following inscription: "When liberty is the prize, Who would shun the warfare? Who would stoop To waste a coward thought on life?" The statue was removed in 1963, when Warren Street was widened, and is now on the campus of the Roxbury Latin School in West Roxbury. (Courtesy of the Gibson House Museum.)

At the dedication of the Warren Monument on June 17, 1904, the invited guests in the official box included Mayor Patrick A. Collins; Henry Putnam, who is addressing the audience; Brigadier General N.A.M. Dudley; Judge Solomon Bolster; Charles T. Gallagher; Dr. Thomas Dwight, who unveiled the statue; Reverend James De Normandie; L. Foster Morse; Samuel Little; F.W. Chandler; Joseph T. Coolidge; Alexander W. Longfellow; C.T. Gallagher; Richard Dwight; W. Prentiss Parker; and M.P. Curran. (Courtesy of the Gibson House Museum.)

Two
The City of Roxbury

The Roxbury Town Hall was built in 1810 and is thought to have been designed by the Boston architect Asher Benjamin. Though it served as the town hall, the Norfolk Guards used the second floor as their armory after their founding in 1818, and a grammar school was conducted here in 1831. After Roxbury was incorporated as a city in 1846, this building served as the city hall and then as a municipal court and police station until 1873, when it was demolished and the Dudley School built on its site. (Courtesy of the West Roxbury Historical Society.)

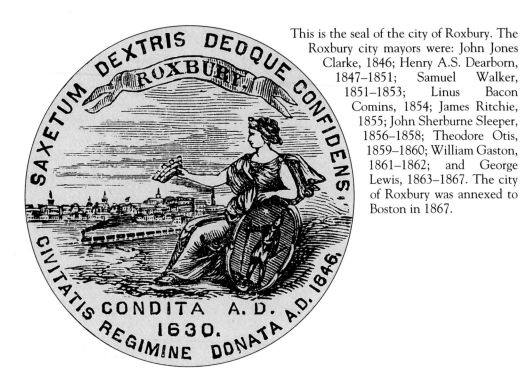

This is the seal of the city of Roxbury. The Roxbury city mayors were: John Jones Clarke, 1846; Henry A.S. Dearborn, 1847–1851; Samuel Walker, 1851–1853; Linus Bacon Comins, 1854; James Ritchie, 1855; John Sherburne Sleeper, 1856–1858; Theodore Otis, 1859–1860; William Gaston, 1861–1862; and George Lewis, 1863–1867. The city of Roxbury was annexed to Boston in 1867.

General Henry A.S. Dearborn (1784–1851) was the second mayor of Roxbury, serving from 1847 to 1851. He was instrumental in the laying out of Forest Hills Cemetery in 1848 and was a president of the Massachusetts Horticultural Society. His estate was at the corner of Tremont and Saint Alphonsus Streets, which later became the site of Mission Church. (Courtesy of the West Roxbury Historical Society.)

William Gaston (1820–1894) served as the mayor of Roxbury in 1861 and 1862, as the mayor of Boston in 1871 and 1872, and as governor of Massachusetts in 1875.

Dove's Corners is the junction of Dudley and Warren Streets and was named for William Dove, whose paint shop was located there. Photographed about 1865, the small painting, tinsmith, and roofing shops would later be replaced by the Hotel Dartmouth and the Dudley Street terminal of the Boston Elevated Railway. (Courtesy of the West Roxbury Historical Society, and thanks to John Cornelius.)

Torrent No. 6 was an engine company located on Eustis Street. Standing in front of the firehouse is William C. Hunneman. This small firehouse was later replaced by a brick firehouse built by John Hall in 1859. On the left can be seen the Eustis Street Burial Ground, laid out in 1633. By 1867, the other Roxbury engine companies were Warren No. 1 (Dudley and Warren Streets), America No. 2 (Centre Street), Torrent No. 5 (Eustis Street), Tremont No. 7 (Cabot Street), and one hook and ladder, Washington No. 1.

Three firemen stand with Warren No. 2, in front of the firehouse that was built in 1864. The fireman on the right leaning on the pumper is James E. Cole. Roxbury Engine No. 3 had no company attached to it and was kept in the gun house behind the town hall. (Courtesy of the West Roxbury Historical Society.)

The Cochituate Stand Pipe was built in 1869 on Fort Hill to store water and pump it to houses in Roxbury. Built on the site of the Roxbury High Fort, it can be seen from miles around. The monument proclaims, "On this eminence stood Roxbury High Fort, a strong earthwork planned by Henry Knox and Josiah Waters and erected by the American Army June, 1776, crowning the famous Roxbury lines of investment at the Siege of Boston." At the urging of the Roxbury Historical Society in 1906, the tower later became an observatory, with panoramic views from all sides at the top of the tower. In 1895, Frederick Law Olmstead was commissioned by the city of Boston to design the surrounding park.

The junction of Dudley and Washington Streets had become a commercial intersection by the 1870s. On the left is the Guild Building, or the Dudley Block, at the corner of Washington Street and Guild Row. At the next corner is the People's and Eliot Savings Banks. The Hotel Dartmouth can be seen in the distance. (Courtesy of William Dillon.)

From the corner of Warren and Dudley Streets, the spire of the Dudley Street Baptist Church rises on the left, and the Hotel Dartmouth and Palladio Hall can be seen on the right. (Courtesy of William Dillon.)

Edward Seaver served as a state senator from Roxbury at the turn of the century. A member of the family for whom Seaver Street was named, he dealt in the development of real estate.

The People's National Bank was at the corner of Washington and Dudley Streets. The bank was incorporated in 1834, nationalized in 1864, and was built on the site of the house of Reverend John Eliot. On the right is the Eliot Savings Bank. (Courtesy of William Dillon.)

Harry L. Burrage served as president of the Eliot Savings Bank in Roxbury at the turn of the century.

Abraham Shuman was known of as "one of Boston's great merchants." His men's and boy's clothing store was at the corner of Washington and Summer Streets, which was known as "Shuman's Corner." He lived at 60 Vernon Street in Roxbury, where he "delights to think that he has done much to make it the creditable place it is to-day."

One of Roxbury's greatest sons was James Michael Curley (1874–1958), shown here with Thomas Norton Hart (right), a former mayor of Boston. Photographed at Boston City Hall in 1923, Curley would be elected mayor of Boston four times. The son of immigrants from Ireland, Curley would later serve in Congress and as governor of Massachusetts.

The Hotel Dartmouth was an apartment hotel built in 1871 at the corner of Washington and Dudley Streets. Designed by John Roulestone Hall, it was a massive building with a modern mansard roof. On the right is Palladio Hall, built and designed by Nathaniel J. Bradlee, who also owned it. Both structures were named to the National Register of Historic Places. (Courtesy of the BPL.)

Michael J. McEttrick served as a congressman from Roxbury, later serving as a state senator. It was said that he believed "the Constitution of the United States guarantees freedom of conscience and freedom of worship to every American citizen, it guarantees with equal right, freedom of education."

The Roxbury Court House, an impressive Georgian Revival structure, was built on Roxbury Street at the site of the old Washington Grammar School.

Solomon Bolster served as justice of the municipal court in Roxbury at the turn of the century. A resident of Cobden Street, he was a prominent attorney before his appointment to the bench.

Caleb Fellows (1771–1852), a wealthy sea captain, bequeathed a legacy to the city of Roxbury that stated, "In order to the extent of my ability, that I may benefit and please the inhabitants of Roxbury in Massachusetts, I propose by this will to provide for an Athenaeum to be established there." (Courtesy of the Fine Arts Department of the Boston Public Library.)

The Fellows Athenaeum was built at the corner of Millmont Street and Lambert Avenue and opened in 1873 with 5,700 books. The Boston Public Library and the Trustees of the Fellows Athenaeum jointly operated the library. Since 1973, the Dudley Street Branch Library has administered the trust bequeathed to the citizens of Roxbury by Caleb Fellows.

Mayor John B. Hynes (1898–1970) reads to a future Boston voter in 1954, following the dedication ceremonies of the Egleston Square Branch of the Boston Public Library. (Courtesy of the BPL.)

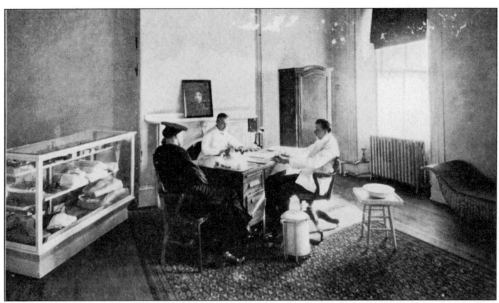

This image shows the medical staff in the Supervisor's Consulting Room at the Salvation Army Roxbury Dispensary in the late 1920s.

Three
Places of Worship

A horse cart crosses Eliot Square in 1890 with the First Parish Church in Roxbury on the left, the Cox Building (built c. 1870) in the center, and Norfolk Hall on the right. Eliot Square was named in memory of Reverend John Eliot (1604–1690), the "Apostle to the Indians" and the first minister of the Roxbury meetinghouse, which first gathered in 1631. The first Sunday school in this country began here in 1674. (Courtesy of William Dillon.)

By the late nineteenth century, the First Parish Church in Roxbury stood opposite the common, with wood plank and granite railings surrounding the tree-shaded knoll. Built in 1804 and designed by William Blaney, the elegant meetinghouse could also boast a bell cast by Paul Revere. (Courtesy of the BPL.)

The gallery in the First Parish Church has a Hooks and Hastings organ (Opus 1171) which was installed in 1883; it was restored by S.L. Huntington & Company and is again "sounding forth in all her high Victorian glory." The galley clock was made by Simon Willard, a member of the congregation and considered the foremost American clockmaker of all time.

Reverend James De Normandie, D.D. (1862–1924), was the pastor of the First Parish Church from 1883 to 1917. He served as a director of the American Unitarian Association and was considered "one of the most eloquent and effective preachers Boston ever had."

The First Parish Church was greatly remodeled at the turn of the century; new ceiling decorations and a classical pulpit were installed.

Edward Everett Hale (1822–1909) addressed members of the First Parish Church after services on July 12, 1908. Hale, a nephew of Governor Edward Everett, served as chaplain of the United States Senate and was the retired minister of the South Congregational Church in Boston. (Courtesy of the BPL.)

The Baptist church in Roxbury was dedicated in 1821. The first pastor was Reverend William Leverett. A typical New England meetinghouse, the building was sold in 1852 and moved to the corner of Warren and Cliff Streets for use as the First Methodist Episcopal Church. The new converts to the Baptist faith were baptized in the Stony Brook River, which attracted great attention from the primarily Unitarian residents.

The Dudley Street Baptist Church, which had officially changed its name in 1850, built a new church in 1852 on Dudley Street near Warren Street. A pointed Gothic-style brick church, it was covered with mastic and blocked off in imitation of brown sandstone. In 1967, the church disbanded and merged with the Centre Street Baptist Church in Jamaica Plain, which is now known as the United Baptist Church.

The "Kimball Class" of the Dudley Street Church was a women's Sunday school class. The club was named for Deacon Edward R. Kimball, who sits in the middle of the second row. The aim of the Kimball Class was "to study God's Word, to promote friendliness among women, and to co-operate in the undertakings of our Church." (Courtesy of William F. Clark.)

"Kimball Class."

The Eliot Congregational Church was built in 1835 on Kenilworth Street. The spire was added in 1847 when the church was considerably enlarged. Unfortunately, this landmark was destroyed by fire in 1953.

The Roxbury Universalist Church was founded in 1821. The first minister was Reverend Hosea Ballou. This meetinghouse was built in 1841 on Guild Row and was enlarged in 1866.

The Saint James' Church, founded in 1832, was built in 1834 on Saint James Street. Built of the famous Roxbury puddingstone, the church is thought to have been designed by Richard Upjohn. The first rector was Reverend Mark Anthony De Wolf Howe, later the Bishop of Pennsylvania.

The nave of Saint James' Church had high vaulted arches with lancet windows.

The Church of the New Jerusalem was built in 1873 at the corner of Warren, Regent, and Saint James Streets. The church motto was "All religion has relation to Life, and the life of religion is to do good." The church became the Church of God in Christ in 1959 and was later demolished in 1985. (Courtesy of William F. Clark.)

The Advent Christian Church, with its publishing house on the first floor, was on Warren Street and was the successor to the Methodist Episcopal Church. The congregation later moved to Washington Street, near Four Corners in Dorchester, and renamed themselves the Greenwood Memorial Church. The church in the photograph is now the Second African Meeting House, Twelfth Baptist Church.

The Walnut Avenue Congregational
Church was founded in 1870. In 1907, the
Walnut Avenue Church and Immanuel
Church (founded in 1857 as the Vine
Street Church) joined congregations.
Today, it is the Eliot Congregational
Church. (Courtesy of William Dillon.)

Reverend Albert H. Plumb, D.D., was
pastor of the Walnut Avenue
Congregational Church for twenty-seven
years. He also served as president of the
Congregational Club of Massachusetts.

At the intersection of Humboldt and Walnut Avenues in 1890, the Walnut Avenue Congregational Church is on the right, and a "three-decker" is on the left. (Courtesy of William Dillon.)

The Roxbury Presbyterian Church was built in 1891 at the corner of Warren and Waverley Streets and was designed by John Calvin Spofford of the Boston architectural firm of Brigham and Spofford. The first minister was Reverend Martin D. Kneeland.

The Freewill Baptist Church was built in 1897 at the corner of Warren and Deckard Streets. Today, it is the Emmanuel Temple Pentecostal Church. (Courtesy of the West Roxbury Historical Society.)

All Souls' Unitarian Church was built in 1888 at the corner of Warren Street and Elm Hill Avenue. Today, the church is the Charles Street African Methodist Church, which was founded in 1833 on Charles Street on the flat of Beacon Hill. (Courtesy of the West Roxbury Historical Society.)

The Elm Hill Baptist Church was a fanciful Shingle-style church in the Elm Hill area of Roxbury. (Courtesy of the West Roxbury Historical Society.)

The Swedish Lutheran Emmanuel Church was built at the corner of Warren Street and Kearsage Avenue in 1923. Today, the Resurrection Lutheran Church worships here. (Courtesy of William F. Clark.)

Saint Mark's Evangelical English Lutheran Church was built on Withrop Street, off Warren Street. The Southern Baptist Church, which was founded in 1960, worships here today. (Courtesy of William F. Clark.)

Saint Patrick's Church was founded in 1872. This church was built at the junction of Dudley and Dunmore Streets and was the third Catholic parish in Roxbury. The first parish was Saint Patrick's, which was founded in 1836 on Northampton Street, and the second parish was Saint Joseph's (often referred to as "Tommy's Rock"), which was founded in 1845 on Circuit Street.

The Convent for Saint Patrick's Church was designed by noted architect Edward T.P. Graham.

Saint Hugh's Church was built in 1901 at 517 Blue Hill Avenue. It was made of granite that was reused when the Masonic Temple at the corner of Tremont and Boylston Streets was demolished. Today, the church is known as Saint John-Saint Hugh's.

The Ruggles Street Baptist Church was organized in 1870. It was a joining of the Branch Chapel Mission and the Ruggles Street Baptist Mission, with Reverend Robert Seymour as the first pastor. The original church was a small wooden church that was enlarged over the years until it was destroyed by fire in 1925. In 1935, a new stone church was dedicated and was used until 1970, when the church moved to Audubon Circle. (Courtesy of William F. Clark.)

Reverend Robert G. Seymour, D.D., was the first pastor of the Ruggles Street Baptist Church. (Courtesy of William F. Clark.)

Adath Jeshuran was a Jewish temple built on Blue Hill Avenue in 1906. The first Jewish temple in Roxbury was Agudas Achem (the Intervale Street Synagogue) in 1894 and was followed by Mishkan Tefila in 1898, Shaare Tefilo (Otisfield Street Synagogue) in 1908, Beth Hamidrash Hagadol (Crawford Street Synagogue) in 1913, and Nusach Sfard (Lawrence Avenue Synagogue) in 1915. Today, Adath Jeshuran is used by the First Haitian Baptist Church of Boston.

Ionic Hall was purchased in 1876 by Saint Luke's Home for Convalescents "to provide shelter and care for such women as the hospitals could not retain after illness." Saint Luke's cared for all in medical need, regardless of creed.

Four
Schools

The Roxbury Latin School was on Kearsage Avenue, off Warren Street. Founded in 1645, the purpose of the school was to fit boys for "public service both in church and Commonwealth in succeeding ages." It would evolve as one of the foremost and oldest preparatory schools in this country.

William Coe Collar, A.M., (1833–1916) was headmaster of the Roxbury Latin School from 1867 to 1907. He was referred to as the "Second Founder," as the school had quadrupled in size during his tenure.

Class I students study in the South Room under the direction of William Coe Collar in 1904.

Pupils of Class V read at their desks, under the supervision of Onsville M. Farnham, in the North Room in 1904.

Students work in the Chemistry Laboratory as N. Henry Black, science master from 1900 to 1924, watches their experiments—intently! Black left Roxbury Latin in 1924 to teach chemistry at Harvard.

The old Roxbury High School was built in 1854 and was a small, three-story schoolhouse of Roxbury puddingstone and granite corner quoining. Students walk past the school on Kenilworth Street in 1871. This building later became the Kenilworth Street Primary School. (Courtesy of the BPL.)

Horace Mann was the man for whom the School for the Deaf was named. The school (now the Phillis Wheatley School) was built in 1932 at 20 Kearsage Avenue, the former site of the Roxbury Latin School. Mann wrote about the schools for the deaf that he visited in Germany in 1843, which led to a greater understanding of the need for these type of schools.

John Kneeland (1821–1914) was a member of the Board of Supervisors of the Boston Public Schools and credited his success as "School, private study, early companionship, home, and contact with men in active life."

Students of the Class of 1892 pose for their class portrait on the steps of the Roxbury High School. The school was built in 1885 on Warren Street. (Courtesy of the BPL.)

Roxbury High School was built in 1885 and designed by Charles J. Bateman and Harrison H. Atwood. A massive Romanesque Revival brick and brownstone school, it had a soaring clock tower that could be seen along Warren Street. The school later became the Boston Clerical School. It was demolished in 1976— a great loss to the streetscape. (Courtesy of William Dillon.)

Harrison H. Atwood (1863–1954) was the architect who completed the Roxbury High School. A successful Boston architect, he also designed numerous other Boston schools, including the Henry L. Pierce and Emily Fifield in Dorchester, the Prince and Saint Botolph Street in the Back Bay, and the Bowditch in Jamaica Plain. He was Boston's city architect from 1889 to 1891 and designed numerous residences, including his own on Alban Street in Dorchester.

A cadre of hungry schoolboys congregate in the cafeteria of the Roxbury High School at the turn of the century. Cafeteria workers provided sandwiches, hot soup, and fruit for the ever-hungry students during their lunch period.

Members of the band at the High School of Practical Arts pose outside the entrance to their school. The high school was built in 1914 at the corner of Winthrop and Greenville Streets and was modeled on the premise of training girls for practical arts, rather than a college course. The entrance to the school was flanked by impressive twin caryatids whose heads support the lintel over the door. (Courtesy of the late Ruth Raycraft.)

Roxbury Memorial High School was built at the corner of Warren and Townsend Streets and was segregated for boys and girls. Later, it was used as Boston Technical High School, and it is currently used as Boston Latin Academy. The Roxbury Memorial Branch of the Boston Public Library was located here for many years. (Courtesy of William F. Clark.)

These young women are members of the Athletic Association of the Roxbury Memorial High School for Girls in 1928. From left to right are as follows: (seated) Sylvia Minnucci, Esther Bassick, Marjorie Spinney, and Michelina Rizzo; (standing) Eunice Lahaise, Muriel Kodis, and Helen Jackson. (Courtesy of Mary A. Connell.)

The Dudley School was founded in 1873 and built on the site of the Roxbury Town Hall. Named for the prominent Dudley family, members included Governor Thomas Dudley (1576–1653), Governor Joseph Dudley (1647–1723), Chief Justice Paul Dudley (1676–1751), and Colonel William Dudley (1636–1743).

A sewing class at the John Winthrop School taught young girls how to use a needle and thread. These sewing teachers were sponsored by Mary Porter Tileston Hemenway (1820–1894), a wealthy woman who extolled the virtues of industrial arts in the Boston Public Schools and personally subsidized the salaries and expenses involved for several years.

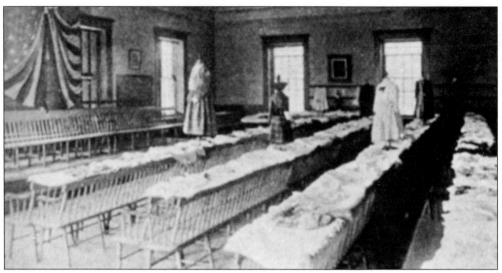

At the turn of the century, Robert Swan was the headmaster of the Winthrop School, located at 35 Brookfield Street. In 1865, he was approached by Mrs. Hemenway, who wanted to see sewing taught to girls from an early age so that they had a vocation upon graduation. Hesitant at first, Swan "furnished a class of girls to be instructed in advance needlework, [and Mrs. Hemenway paid] all expenses for materials and teachers."

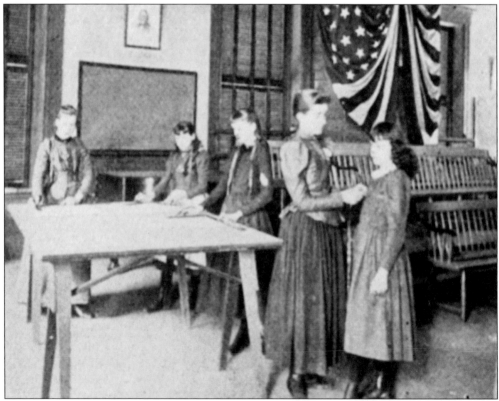

Girls stand at the cutting table and trace patterns onto cloth that would be cut later and basted for a garment.

Mrs. Hemenway was in favor of cooking classes as well. Here, students listen to their teacher's directions in a cooking class at the Winthrop School in 1899.

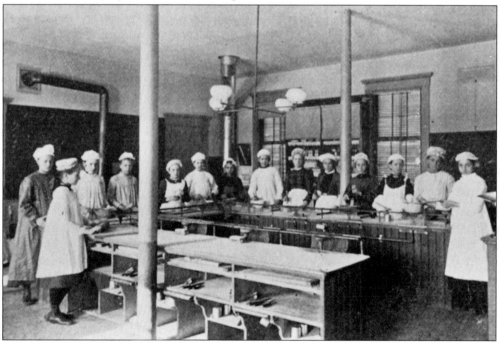

Students in a cooking class at the Winthrop School were taught in twelve lessons how to prepare and cook a wholesome and nourishing dinner. After portions of a dinner were prepared by the girls at home, they were brought to class, and a school dinner was held to sample the girls' "lessons." Started at the Winthrop School, the industrial arts course was eventually expanded to other schools in the system.

Students at the George Putnam Grammar School, 2025 Columbus Avenue, prepare beds in which to cultivate vegetables. The school was named in honor of Reverend Putnam, pastor of the First Church from 1830 to 1878, who served twenty-five years on the Roxbury School Committee and forty-five years as president of the trustees of the Roxbury Latin School.

Teachers and parents watch the students plant seeds that will eventually grow into vegetables. This experiment showed the students, many of whom had never before worked in a garden, the many advantages of growing, weeding, and cultivating plants.

These girls are planting seeds in the prepared beds.

A remarkably well-dressed student, complete with a straw bonnet, weeds a vegetable patch in the George Putnam Grammar School garden. These experimental gardens eventually led to the Victory Gardens that were cultivated during World War I and World War II.

The Boston Public Schools are named after people who have made contributions to the well being of the community and in recognition of their accomplishments. The Phillis Wheatley Middle School, originally the Horace Mann, was renamed after Phillis Wheatley (1753?–1784), a "Negro Servant to Mr. John Wheatley, of Boston" and author of the book *Poems on Various Subjects, Religious and Moral*, which was published in 1773.

William Monroe Trotter (1872–1934) was a graduate of Harvard, where he was the first African-American Phi Beta Kappa and a founder of the Niagra Movement, the precursor of the NAACP. For thirty-three years he was the editor of *The Guardian*, a Boston newspaper for the African-American community. A school was named after him on Humboldt Avenue in 1969.

The Elm Hill School was founded by Alice Collar Davis, daughter of Headmaster Collar of the Roxbury Latin School. Located on Wenonah Street, Elm Hill was housed in Fauntleroy Hall, a low Shingle-style schoolhouse designed by Edwin J. Lewis Jr., where it provided intermediate, general, and college preparatory courses until 1915. (Courtesy of William F. Clark.)

The Weston School for Girls was a private academy for young ladies at 37–43 Saint James Street. A day and resident school, it fitted young ladies "for life as well as examinations."

Notre Dame Academy was located at 2893 Washington Street in a large convent school operated by the Sisters of Notre Dame.

The chapel of Notre Dame Academy was an elegant barrel-vaulted room with a white marble altar at the end of the nave. In Latin, around the arch, was "Ave Maria Gratia Plena Dominus Tecum."

Five
Grove Hall

Looking south on Blue Hill Avenue (originally known as Grove Hall Avenue), one can see that Grove Hall is the junction of Geneva Avenue and Washington Street (on the left). Named for the estate of Thomas Kilby Jones, Grove Hall was built in 1800 at the junction of Washington Street and Blue Hill Avenue. The area became an important center for commerce by the late nineteenth century and was built up with large apartment buildings in the early twentieth century. (Courtesy of William Dillon.)

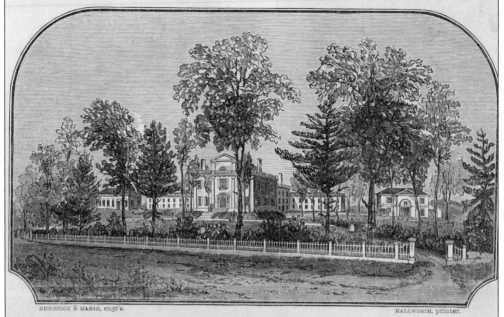
Grove Hall was remodeled by Dr. Alanson Abbe for use as the American Orthopedic Institute in 1848. The mansion, seen just past the trees, was located "one mile from the City of Boston. Its beauty and salubrity is not surpassed, being free from the contaminating influence of a dense population always prejudicial to invalids."

Dr. Charles Cullis founded the Cullis Consumptives' Home in the former institute of Dr. Abbe. A home for incurables, it depended wholly on the kindness and generosity of those who realized what valuable service it rendered. Cullis remodeled the former Grove Hall by removing the front staircase and adding a mansard roof. After these changes to the home, the building was able to care for eighty patients.

Dr. Charles Cullis founded the Consumptives' Home in 1864 and incorporated it in 1870. It was founded in memory of his wife, who had died from consumption in 1862. Cullis based the operation of his home on faith work and had a large sign mounted over the entrance that proclaimed, "Have Faith in God!"

The junction of Warren Street and Blue Hill Avenue at Grove Hall shows a streetcar on the Warren Street Line. Blocks of stores had been built along Blue Hill Avenue, and on the right was the car barn for the street railway. (Courtesy of William Dillon.)

John Calvin Spofford was an architect who designed a large number of houses in Roxbury at the turn of the century. A partner in Brigham and Spofford, he designed the Roxbury Presbyterian Church, the station at Roxbury Crossing on the New York, New Haven, and Hartford Lines, and over forty elegant houses in "Boston Highlands."

Ferdinand Abraham was one of the successful merchants who immigrated from Germany and settled in Roxbury. A dealer in meerschaum goods, he became one of the largest purveyors of pipes in New England. When not occupied at his shop, he served as the president of the Roxbury Bicycle Club and was a member of Temple Adath Israel.

By the early twentieth century, a four-story commercial block was built at the junction of Warren Street and Blue Hill Avenue. A streetcar approaches from Warren Street as a man crosses Blue Hill Avenue near the car barn of the street railway.

Grove Hall Station was on Blue Hill Avenue, opposite Warren Street. Streetcars were parked here overnight, and two streetcars can be seen leaving the car barn in the morning to begin their route.

Though Grove Hall was commercial in nature, the streets leading from it were residential. In 1949, Otto and Muriel Snowdon founded "Freedom House," which was known as Upper Roxbury's Civic Center. Two volunteers operated the membership table for a 1954 campaign for new members. Freedom House, formerly the Hebrew Teachers College, is located on Crawford Street, just off Grove Hall.

Six
Boston Highlands

Alvah Kittredge's mansion was an impressive Greek Revival house that was built in 1836 and set on an extensive tract of land that was being subdivided by the 1870s, as seen on the right. Kittredge was a deacon of the First Parish Church and obviously lived a comfortable life, as this photograph can attest. The house, once facing Highland Street, was surrounded by gardens and had an observatory on the left. In 1871, it became the home of Nathaniel J. Bradlee, a partner in the architectural firm of Bradlee and Winslow. Today, the house is used by the Roxbury Action Program. (Courtesy of the BPL.)

The Williams House, shown here in 1876, was a pleasant country house shaded by massive elm trees. (Courtesy of the BPL.)

Number 119 Dale Street was a Gothic Revival cottage set on a small lot of land. In the period of Roxbury's incorporation as a city, many of these small wood-framed houses were built by the new residents moving from Boston. (Courtesy of the BPL.)

"Rockledge" was the home of William Lloyd Garrison (1805–1879) and was set on a knoll at 125 Highland Street. Since 1900, the house has been operated as Saint Monica's, a nursing home run by the Sisters of Saint Margaret for elderly African-Americans. This is fitting since Garrison had been the founder of the New England Anti-Slavery Society and was the editor of *The Liberator*, Boston's fiery abolitionist newspaper. (Courtesy of the BPL.)

William Lloyd Garrison (left) and Wendell Phillips were among the most outspoken of the members of the anti-slavery cause in Boston. Photographed about 1860, their motto might have been "Whether in Chains or in Laurels, Liberty Knows Nothing but Victories," as they lived to see their ardent wishes granted when Lincoln signed the "Emancipation Proclamation" in 1863.

The Williams House was on Perrin Street, opposite Alaska Street, and it was built just after the Civil War with a then fashionable mansard roof. Photographed in May 1888, members of the Williams family pose for their photograph on the side lawn. (Courtesy of the Williams Family.)

Robert B. Williams (1829–1911) lived at 37 (now 67) Perrin Street and was a Boston merchant who dealt in tea. (Courtesy of the Williams Family.)

Three boys stand at the corner of Alaska and Perrin Streets about 1890. The house behind them is a fine example of the type of houses built in Roxbury in the late nineteenth century. (Courtesy of the Williams Family.)

Looking northeast from the roof of Dr. Day's house (now 69 Perrin Street), one can see the rear wing of the Williams House in the foreground. Toward the corner of Moreland and Copeland Streets, the spire of the Moreland Street Congregational Church rises on the left. The Moreland Street Church was designed by J.H. Besarick and was built in 1886. It was occupied by Temple Mishkan Tefila from 1907 to 1924. (Courtesy of the Williams Family.)

Dr. Frank E. Green lived in this Queen Anne extravaganza at the corner of Waverley and Perrin Streets. Photographed about 1890, the house was that of a prosperous resident of the "Streetcar Suburbs" of Boston. (Courtesy of the Williams Family.)

Brookledge was the home of James I. Brooks and was built on Walnut Avenue in 1892. This street was opposite an entrance to Franklin Park and had large, well-designed houses that fronted onto Olmstead's green space. Brooks was president of the J.I. Brooks & Company, investment bankers in Boston.

Walnut Park, now often referred to as Monroe Park, was bounded by Townsend, Walnut, Harold, and Elmore Streets. In the center of the park, there was a large outcropping of Roxbury puddingstone that was left untouched. Two children sit on a park bench about 1895. (Courtesy of William Dillon.)

William Alfred Paine (1855–1930) was a founder in 1880 of Paine, Webber & Company, a Boston investment house. He lived at 409 Walnut Avenue and was a member and treasurer of the Walnut Avenue Congregational Church, even after he moved to a townhouse on Commonwealth Avenue in the Back Bay.

Elm Hill Avenue connects Warren and Seaver Streets and was named after Elm Hill, the estate of Rufus Greene Amory. By the 1880s, Elm Hill Avenue was built up with commodious houses, many of which were designed by architects. The row of trees along the former carriage drive to Elm Hill survived as late as 1895. (Courtesy of William Dillon.)

The junction of Humboldt Avenue and Crawford Street was photographed about 1895, showing large houses that had been built in Roxbury over the last decade. (Courtesy of William Dillon.)

Charles Follen Adams (1842–1918) was known as "Yawcob Strauss," a writer of German dialect stories for the *Detroit Free Press*. His home was at 59 Waverley Street, where he wove tales about "Dot Leedle Loueeze" and "Leedle Yawcob Strauss," named for his children Ella and Charles Adams. His book *Leedle Yawcob Strauss & Other Poems* (1877) was followed by *Dialect Ballads* (1888).

John Rogers (1829–1904), known as the "People's Sculptor" and producer of "Rogers Groups," was raised on Cedar Street. Rogers' "conversation groups" were cast in plaster with such themes as "Rip Van Winkle," "Coming to the Parson," "The Apostle Eliot," and "The Emancipation Proclamation."

Maurice Brazil Prendergast (1858–1924) was a noted painter who lived at 119 Centre Street from 1880 until 1893. His art was an impressionistic style of painting that attempted to capture a brief, immediate emotion or idea.

Many of the rowhouses being built just after Roxbury was annexed to Boston had marble facades, such as this block between 28 and 46 Cedar Street about 1870. Emulating the townhouses of the South End and Back Bay, they were smaller in size but are important examples of urban architecture in "Boston Highlands." (Courtesy of the BPL.)

The Warren was a six-story apartment building at the junction of Warren and Regent Streets. Built of brick, with limestone stringcourses, it was the home of professionals and young married couples who had not yet purchased a home. On the right is the New Jerusalem Church at the corner of Saint James Street. (Courtesy of William Dillon.)

Some of the apartment buildings along Warren Street were small in comparison to the Warren. The Hotel Holmes (three units at 337 Warren Street), the Hotel Mabel (three units at 331 Warren Street), and the Hotel Margaret (six units at 325 Warren Street) were typical apartment houses with shops on the first floor. (Courtesy of William Dillon.)

As Roxbury estates were subdivided for development, some of the large houses became hospitals and retirement homes. The Mount Pleasant Home for Aged Men and Women, a former mansion, was at 59 Elm Hill Avenue and provided care for the aged poor.

By the turn of the century, the "Three-Decker" had been introduced as a housing style which offered separate apartments with a rear porch and windows on all four sides. These particularly well-designed houses were built at 121 (left) and 119 Dale Street about 1890. (Courtesy of the BPL.)

Seven

Parker Hill and Mission Hill

The view of Boston from Parker Hill was as superb in 1838 as it is today. A cow grazes in the foreground, and the houses of early-nineteenth-century Roxbury cluster at the foot of Parker Hill. The marshes of the "Back Bay" have not yet been filled in for the new neighborhood that was named after the "back bay," and the dome of the Massachusetts State House crowns a densely built Beacon Hill.

John Parker (1757–1840) was a member of the family for whom Parker Hill was named. Parker's mansion stood on the south slope of Parker Hill and was on land that had been owned by the family since 1752. A wealthy merchant, his portrait was painted by Gilbert Stuart, who lived in Roxbury during the War of 1812. (Courtesy of The Boston Athenaeum.)

Parker Hill, known as "Great Hill" in the seventeenth century, had large deposits of Roxbury puddingstone that were quarried for building material in the mid-nineteenth century. Coleman's Quarry, photographed here about 1878, was on Tremont Street, opposite the Mission Church. (Courtesy of the BPL.)

Thomas Thacher (1795–1863) was a merchant and railroad president whose estate was on Alleghaney Street. He was the founder and president of the Fulton Iron Works in South Boston, and devoted both time and effort to the subdivision of his estate, which he began as early as 1845.

The Back Bay, seen from Parker Hill in 1878, was steadily being filled in after it was begun in 1858. On the right can be seen the Mission Church, which was designed for the Redemptionist Fathers by the New York architectural firm Schickel and Detmars, and the orchards on the eastern slope of Parker Hill. (Courtesy of the BPL.)

The Brinley Mansion was at the corner of Tremont and Saint Alphonsus Streets. It was built in 1732 and known as the "Datchet House," after Datchet, England, where the Brinleys had once lived. This mansion was the estate of the Dearborn family before it was purchased by the Redemptionist Fathers. The building on the right with arched windows served as the first church, and the rectory for the priests serving at Mission Church was in the house on the left. (Courtesy of the BPL.)

The original Mission Church was built in 1871 and was a simple wood-framed chapel. The Miraculous Picture, above the altar, was later placed in the Shrine of the present church; the Holy Family (on the left) and Saint Patrick's Altars were later moved to Saint Gerard's Chapel. (Courtesy of Mission Church.)

Reverend Joseph Wissel, C.S.S.R., was the first rector of Mission Church, serving during 1870 and 1871. The Redemptionist Fathers founded Mission Church in 1869 and came from Brooklyn, New York, to serve the many Catholic German immigrants, and later the Irish families, that came to work at the breweries. (Courtesy of Mission Church.)

The present Mission Church was built in 1877 on Tremont Street and was made of Roxbury puddingstone and Quincy granite. To the left is the church that was built in 1871, and on the far left is the Datchet House, the former Dearborn Mansion. The Shrine of Our Lady of Perpetual Help was where the crippled fervently prayed for a cure; crutches and leg braces cover the walls of this shrine from those whose prayers were answered. (Courtesy of Mission Church.)

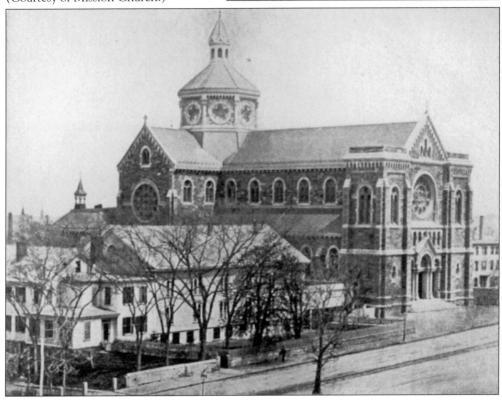

The twin granite towers were added to the Basilica of Our Lady of Perpetual Help (Mission Church) in 1910 by architect Franz Joseph Untersee. Their soaring pinnacles can be seen from all parts of Boston. On the left can be seen the Parochial Residence, built in 1902 on the site of the Datchet House. (Courtesy of Mission Church.)

The banner of Our Lady of Perpetual Help, an exact copy of the original in the church of Saint Alphonsus on via Merulana in Rome, hangs above the marble altar at the end of the nave of Mission Church. The soaring vaulted ceiling and side arches supported by composite columns make for a dramatic and impressive space. (Courtesy of Mission Church.)

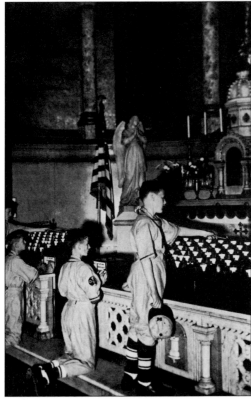

Four baseball players pray and light candles at Mission Church in the 1950s. One wonders if they're praying for a win! (Courtesy of the BPL.)

Saint Alphonsus' Hall was designed by Franz Joseph Untersee and built on Smith Street in 1898, where it was the site of numerous entertainments, theatricals, and plays by members of Mission Church. (Courtesy of Mission Church.)

The Foyer of Saint Alphonsus' Hall had portraits of three presidents of the United States above the entrance doors. From the left are portraits of Thomas Jefferson, George Washington, and Andrew Jackson. A painting by Roab of *Veronica Showing the Towel to the Blessed Virgin* hangs on the left, and the ticket booth is on the right. (Courtesy of Mission Church.)

The 1905 cast of *Pilate's Daughter* poses on the stage of Saint Alphonsus' Hall for a group photograph. The play was written by Reverend F.L. Kenzel in 1901 and performed annually; "the announcement of this church play has become as welcome as the very early spring flowers." Those who participated in the play "acted more as if the play was a religious devotion than a theatrical production." (Courtesy of the BPL.)

The Mission Church Field Band was organized in 1900. Parish priests and members of the band pose for a photograph about 1910. (Courtesy of Mission Church.)

Mission Church also had recreation rooms for members of the parish. Here, a group of men play cards, while others could play billiards or exercise in the gymnasium. Mission Church was not just a place to worship, it was also a place for social activities. (Courtesy of Mission Church.)

By 1915, the view from Parker Hill toward Boston had changed dramatically from the earlier print of 1838. The Back Bay fill-in project was complete by 1900, and numerous "three-deckers" had been built on the former orchards on Parker Hill's slope. The twin spires of Mission Church, added in 1911, rise above the densely settled neighborhood of three-deckers and act as a beacon for all who looked toward "Mission Hill," as the area had become known. (Courtesy of the New England Baptist Hospital.)

The New England Baptist Hospital was founded in 1893; three years later, it moved to the former Bond Mansion on Parker Hill Avenue, at the crest of Parker Hill. An impressive Italianate mansion with a cupola that supplied superb views of the countryside, the Bond House served as the hospital until 1924. (Courtesy of the New England Baptist Hospital.)

Dr. Francis Fremont Whittier (1852–1937) was the founder in 1893 of the Boston Baptist Hospital, which was later renamed the New England Baptist Church.

In the early years of the hospital, tents were used as additional space for patients being treated at the New England Baptist Hospital. These tents, referred to as the "Field Hospital," catered to typhoid and consumption patients from April through November, and the clean air of Parker Hill helped to cure them. A nurse poses beside a tent as a patient sits "taking the air." (Courtesy of the New England Baptist Hospital.)

The Haskell House for Nurses was designed by Edward Sears Rand and opened in 1924 for nurses at the hospital. Named for Colonel Edward H. Haskell (1845–1924), second president of the hospital, the nurse's school emphasized "classroom education and practical, hands-on patient care." These nurses posed for a group photograph in 1940. (Courtesy of the New England Baptist Hospital.)

The original building of the New England Baptist Hospital (left) and the Nurses' Home provided health care to all people, regardless of their ability to pay. (Courtesy of the New England Baptist Hospital.)

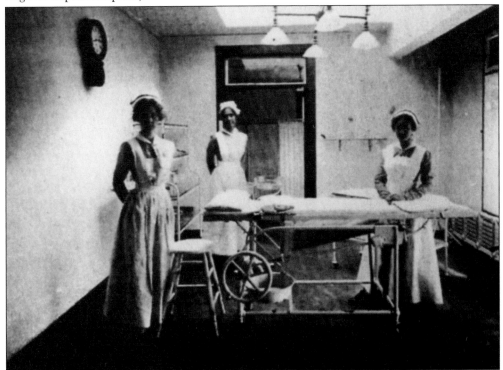

The Operating Room at the New England Baptist Hospital in 1915 was a far cry from the modern facilities available today. Three nurses stand beside a table that was used during operations. (Courtesy of the New England Baptist Hospital.)

The Information Desk in the Main Building (which was designed by Edward Seard Rand and built between 1923 and 1924) was where one could obtain news or directions to patients' rooms. Dr. Robert J. MacMillan, retired chief of staff, stands in the center wearing a bow tie, and Dr. Ross is speaking with Mrs. Henning. Dr. Gary Kearney is on the right in the background. (Courtesy of the New England Baptist Hospital.)

Some patients were thought so special that even television stars visited them while recuperating at the New England Baptist Hospital. Here, Rin Tin Tin sits on a sofa while visiting a young patient in 1956. (Courtesy of the New England Baptist Hospital.)

The Nurse's Clubhouse of the New England Hospital for Women and Children was in a small mansard-roofed cottage on Dimock Street. Dr. Susan Dimock founded the hospital in 1860 in reaction to the exclusion of women in medicine and also to care for indigent women and children. In 1875, the first professional school of nursing in this country was opened here.

Shown here sitting on the lawn at the Public Health Hospital on Parker Hill about 1920 are, from left to right, Misses Stevens, Stanley, and Glastridge, Mrs. Freeman, Mrs. Morgan, Miss Roberts, and the gentlemen patients of the hospital.

The Robert Breck Brigham Hospital was built in 1914 on Parker Hill Avenue. Named for the man whose fortune endowed the hospital, it was an impressive hospital designed by Shepley, Rutan, and Coolidge. The hospital was purchased by the New England Baptist Hospital in 1969 and is now the Brigham, Fogg, and Fremont-Smith Buildings. (Courtesy of the New England Baptist Hospital.)

The Peter Bent Brigham Hospital is an impressive colonnaded building that was designed by Codman & Espadrille and built in 1913 at the junction of Huntington Avenue and Francis Street. Named for a generous benefactor, the uncle of Robert Breck Brigham, the hospital lent its name to the intersection in the foreground, Brigham Circle. Today, the hospital is part of Brigham & Women's Hospital.

Eight
Business and Industry

J.G. & B.S. Ferguson was a wholesale bakery at 869 Albany Street. A convoy of horse-drawn delivery wagons are in front of the bakery awaiting baked goods that will be delivered throughout Boston to grocery stores, restaurants, hotels, and caterers.

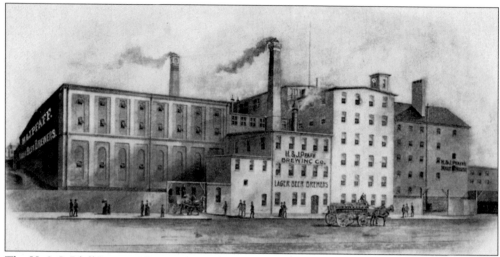

The H. & J. Pfaff Brewing Company was located on Pynchon Street (now Columbus Avenue). Founded in 1857, the brewery specialized in lager beer, a beer that must be aged for several months.

Henry Pfaff was one of the founders, in 1857, of H. & J. Pfaff Brewing Company, with his brother, Jacob Pfaff.

A man stands beside machinery in the Engine Room of the H. & J. Pfaff Brewing Company.

Colonel Charles Pfaff was president of the H. & J. Pfaff Brewing Company at the turn of the century. He also served as president of the Massachusetts Breweries Company.

The brewery of A.J. Houghton Company was founded in 1876 on Station Street. The Houghton Company specialized in "Vienna" and "Pavonia" Lager Beer and had the capacity to produce 100,000 barrels of beer a year. Two horse teams pulling barrels of lager pass in front of the brewery in 1895.

Andrew Jackson Houghton (1827–1901) was the founder of the A.J. Houghton Company.

The Engine Room of the A.J. Houghton Company was a two-story room that housed the machinery used in the brewing of their lager beers.

Louis Prang (1824–1909) introduced "chromos," or reproductions of oil paintings by a process called chromo-lithography, at his factory in Roxbury. Compelled to leave Germany in 1848, as he was an advocate of social democracy, Prang used his extensive knowledge of colors to begin his printing concern. He invented the Prang method of art instruction, used in the Boston Public Schools for many years.

Louis Prang's Art Publishing House had opened in Roxbury in 1856 and was considered "the most extensive of its kind in the country, and it is to the credit of Boston that the reputation of the chromos produced here is not inferior to that of any others."

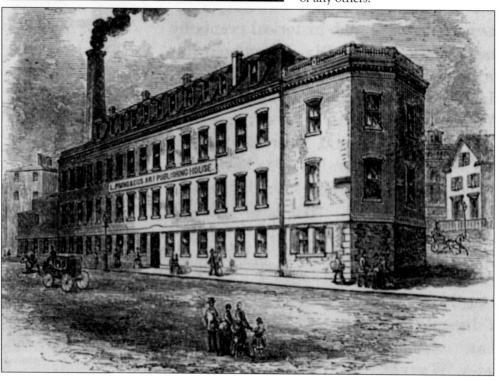

Prang introduced the Christmas card to this country in 1875, a year after it had appeared in England. These cards were small works of art and showcase the "care with which each stone must be prepared, every one adding one color, and only one, to the picture that is by and by to appear; the successive steps by which apparently shapeless patches of color are transformed into excellent and artistic imitations of well-known oil paintings."

Louis Prang's skill and success as a chromo-lithographer enabled him to build this fashionable house at 45 Centre Street, overlooking the factory, which can be seen on the left. (Courtesy of the BPL.)

Simon Willard (1753–1848) is considered the foremost American clockmaker of all time. Born in Grafton, Massachusetts, Simon and his three brothers, Benjamin, Aaron, and Ephriam, were all clockmakers. He moved to Roxbury in 1780 and produced the first banjo clock ("Willard Patent Timepiece") in this country, and the style of his tall case clocks became known as Roxbury cases. Photographed at an advanced age, he holds an ivory-tipped cane that was presented to him by President Thomas Jefferson.

On the left, at the turn of the century, was Simon Willard's house and clock shop on Washington Street. On the right is the house of Mr. Child.

Francis Jackson Ward (1830–1912) was known as "Boney" Ward for his rendering of horses on Spectacle Island. The business had been started by his father, Nahum Ward, in 1828 as a tallow chandlery on Ward Street in Roxbury. It grew to such proportions that it was moved to Spectacle Island, which had been purchased by the family in 1857, to the relief of his neighbors living downwind. In 1896, the business was sold to the American Glue Company.

Hunneman & Company produced the first American suction engine in 1833 on Hunneman Street in Roxbury. William C. Hunneman had built a tub in 1822, known as "The Phillips," which was used to fight fires with water that filled from fire buckets, but the later Hunneman steamers proved to be not only more efficient but an advanced form of firefighting. (Courtesy of the West Roxbury Historical Society.)

W. & A. Bacon was established in 1814 and was considered the oldest dry goods store in Boston at the turn of the century. Located at 2193 Washington Street, its motto was "Your Grandmother Traded Here." (Courtesy of William F. Clark.)

This interior view of A.D. Mowry & Company's Pharmacy reveals a well-stocked apothecary shop that filled not just prescriptions but also had a "hot and cold" fountain for beverages on the right. Located at 329 Warren Street, Mowry's also carried confectionaries, stationery, fancy soaps, toiletries, fancy goods, and perfumes. (Courtesy of William Dillon.)

Ferdinand and Company was a furniture store that was "opened by a sailor home from the sea" at the corner of Washington and Warren Streets. Photographed in 1869, rolled carpets and household furnishings are displayed along the sidewalk. (Courtesy of William Clark.)

By the turn of the century, Frank Ferdinand had built the "Blue Store" on the site of his father's shop. Founded in 1865, it was "one of the largest concerns in the city handling furniture, carpets, stoves, bedding, and house-furnishing goods."

Frank S. Waterman, with his brother, George H. Waterman, carried on the undertaking business, or "coffin warerooms," that had been started in 1832 by his father, Joseph Sampson Waterman. Today, the firm is known as J.S. Waterman & Sons-Eastman-Waring, and is the oldest purveyor of funeral services in Boston.

The Planing Mill and Shop of Morrison & Rackley was at 167 and 169 Dudley Street. These builders and contractors put up a great number of the houses built in Roxbury in the late nineteenth century.

The Power House of the Suburban Light and Power Company was on Norfolk Avenue.

The Dynamo Room of the Suburban Light and Power Company was where electricity was generated for the illumination of residences and businesses.

The Boston Belting Company was on Elmwood Street and was the oldest, and among the largest, works in the world involved in the manufacture of rubber goods. Employing an average of six hundred workers, the plant spread over 3 acres near Roxbury Crossing.

The Kidder Press Manufacturing Company was on Norfolk Avenue and provided the design and construction of all kinds of printing machinery.

A group of workers operate machinery in the plant of J.M. Marston & Company, on Columbus Avenue at the corner of Ruggles Street. The plant manufactured Marston's Patent Hand and Foot and Steam Power Machinery and also a wide variety of machine works.

John M. Marston established his machinery company in 1844 and lived at 30 Greenville Street.

The yard and teams of Nawn &
Company were at 82 Savin
Street, now the corner of
Washington Street and Melnea
Cass Boulevard.

Hugh Nawn was a general
contractor and quarry man who
established his contracting
business in Roxbury just after the
Civil War. His son, Henry P.
Nawn, continued the business
and greatly expanded it.

Nine
Transportation

Roxbury Crossing was formerly known as Pierpont's Village, which was named after the gristmill that stood at Tremont Street and Columbus Avenue (where the railroad station was). The station of the New York, New Haven and Hartford Railroad Lines that was designed by John Calvin Spofford can be seen on the right, before the grade crossing was changed. Two streetcars pass on the right, and the bustling area of factories and breweries can be seen in the distance. (Courtesy of William Dillon.)

David Claypool Johnston (1798–1865) produced a watercolor of the Providence Railroad as it went through Roxbury about 1855, connecting Boston and Providence, Rhode Island. Johnston, who lived in Roxbury between 1854 and 1859, was a noted political cartoonist whose satirical art attracted nationwide attention.

The Highland Railway Station was the terminus for the horse-drawn streetcars that serviced Roxbury in the late nineteenth century.

A streetcar passes the corner of Warren and Rockland Streets in 1893. This streetcar line connected Franklin Street in Boston with Grove Hall in Roxbury via Washington and Warren Streets. (Courtesy of the Williams Family.)

A streetcar approaches Eliot Square from Dudley Street about 1895. On the left is Roxbury Street, and the spire of the First Parish Church can be seen rising above the trees.

Julius E. Rugg was the inventor of the "Rugg Car-seat," a reversible car seat that was adopted by nearly every street railway in this country at the turn of the century. Rugg, a resident of Roxbury, also "organized the first beneficial society designed exclusively for the conductors and drivers of street railways, which has proved of great benefit to the men and their families."

The Dudley Street Terminal of the Boston Elevated Railway was built in 1901 and was designed by Alexander Wadsworth Longfellow. It served as the terminus until the line was extended to Forest Hills in 1909. The station serviced both streetcars and trains on the Elevated Railway. The highly decorative station, with diamond-paned clerestory windows and a sweeping copper roof, has been preserved as a waiting station for buses servicing the area.

The Dudley Street Terminal had a circular loop, seen on the right, for the reversing of the passenger coach. The waiting platforms for passengers were on either side of the central station.

William A. Bancroft was the first president of the Boston Elevated Railway Company, which began as a three-car electric train in June of 1901.

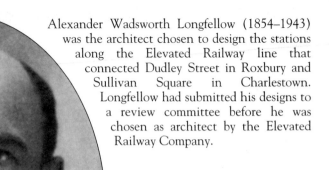

Alexander Wadsworth Longfellow (1854–1943) was the architect chosen to design the stations along the Elevated Railway line that connected Dudley Street in Roxbury and Sullivan Square in Charlestown. Longfellow had submitted his designs to a review committee before he was chosen as architect by the Elevated Railway Company.

On August 4, 1910, a train at the Dudley Street Terminus jumped the track and lodged on a roof adjacent to the Eliot Savings Bank. One person was killed, and the extent of the damage was estimated at $50,000.

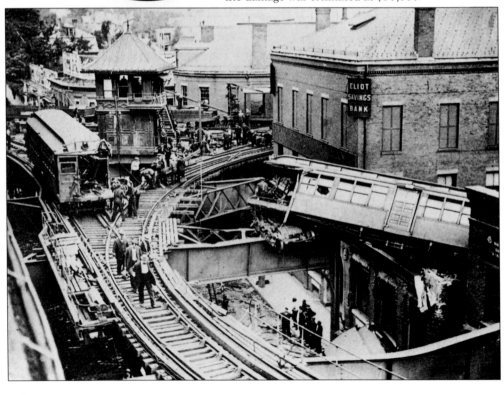

This group is celebrating fifty years of employment with the Boston Elevated Company in 1927. They are, from left to right, as follows: (seated) Patrick Roach, James Kenney, A.L. Hauser, John Howard, Patrick Horan, William Pett, James Smith, Timothy Connell, Andrew Blake, Henry Bryant, Patrick Kelly, George Clark, and John Sullivan; (standing) F.E. Hanington, C.H. Lewis, Robert Nelson, Patrick Donoghue, Richard Moore, T. Devine, Frank Holbrook, John Carl, C.I. Chadbourne, Frank Brown, Charles Seaver, George Costello, Austin Shuttleworth, and George Gilman.

A train heads inbound toward Northampton Station on the Boston Elevated Railway. The "El" ran above Washington Street, the former "Neck" that connected Boston to the mainland at Roxbury. The El was dismantled between 1975 and 1976, after serving passengers for seventy-five years.

The origin of the Flood of 1886 could be seen looking from Linden Park. A large group of people stand on high land and gaze in disbelief at the depth of the water. An outlet that entered the sewer at the corner of Whittier and Tremont Streets could not dispose of the water fast enough, and water eventually rose to a height of 3 feet in places. (Courtesy of William F. Clark.)

Belmont Street was flooded to the depth of 2 feet, and residents used small boats to leave their houses. Belmont Street connected Ruggles and Vernon Streets, and in 1886, it was renamed Haskins Street, in honor of Reverend Haskins of Saint Francis de Sales Church on Vernon Street. Many of the residents were employed in the businesses affected by the flood. Among them were the Boston Belting, Roxbury Carpet, Tower Oil Clothing, Whittier Machine, and Chubbuck Machine Companies. (Courtesy of William F. Clark.)

Ten

The Great Flood
of 1886

In February 1886, a group of people stand on either side of Ruggles Street after the flood that swamped the area bounded by Shawmut Avenue and Lenox, Tremont, and Roxbury Streets. After three days of continuous rain and the addition of melting snow and ice, the water could not run off quickly enough and consequently flooded 63 acres to a depth of 3 feet. The Flood of 1886 was photographed by Baldwin Coolidge, a Boston photographer. (Courtesy of William F. Clark.)

The home of the Honorable Linus Bacon Comins, a former mayor of Roxbury, was flooded by water on all sides, which made the family virtual prisoners in their home until the water subsided. (Courtesy of William F. Clark.)

At the corner of Cabot and Ruggles Streets, the water created a veritable sea in front of a house that served as a kindergarten and nursing society for training young women. The brick tower of Saint Francis de Sales Church rises in the background. (Courtesy of William F. Clark.)

Rowhouses facing Madison Park, which was between Marble, Warwick, Westminster and Sterling Streets, were inaccessible due to the depth of the water. It was reported that over nine hundred houses had been affected by the flood waters, inconveniencing over three thousand residents. (Courtesy of William F. Clark.)

The rear of the rowhouses on Madison Park back up to the flood. The water took several days to subside. (Courtesy of William F. Clark.)

Acknowledgments

I would like to extend my sincere thanks to William F. Clark, a past president of the Roxbury Historical Society, for his interest, generosity of time, and in the loaning of many of the photographs used in this pictorial history of Roxbury, Massachusetts. Without his involvement, it would not have been possible.

I would like to thank the following for their assistance in researching this book, and their continued support and interest: Daniel J. Ahlin, Edmund and Carol Tobin Blake, Anthony Bognanno, Paul and Helen Graham Buchanan, Jamie Carter, Janice Chadbourne of the Fine Arts Department of the Boston Public Library, Elizabeth Williams Clapp, Mary G. Connell, John D. Cornelius, Reverend Elizabeth Curtiss, Elsie De Normandie, Dexter, William Dillon, Catherine Flannery, the Gibson House Museum, Edward W. Gordon, James Green, Virginia Holbrook, Martha Horsefield, Constance Rogers Hsia, Frank Kirchthurn (past president of the Roxbury Historical Society), James Z. Kyprianos, the late Veronica M. Lehane, Susan Lovell, Barbara Martin, Robert J. Mac Millan (M.D.), Jonathan T. Melick, Barbara J. Mulville, the New England Baptist Hospital, Stephen and Susan Paine, William H. Pear, Mary Moran Perry, the late Ruth Raycraft, Joan Regal, Alan H. Robbins (M.D. and president of the New England Baptist Hospital), David Rooney, the late Francis Russell, Dennis Ryan, Anthony and Mary Mitchell Sammarco, Rosemary Sammarco, Sylvia Sandeen, Robert Bayard Severy, Joyce Stevens of Heritage Education, Janice Sullivan, Carolyn Thornton, William Varrell, Virginia M. White, Constance Williams, L. Ware Williams, Susan Williams, Elaine James (Branch Librarian) and her staff at the Dudley Street Branch of the Boston Public Library, and Jacquelyn Hogan (Branch Librarian) and her staff at the Grove Hall Branch of the Boston Public Library.

A portion of the royalties from this book will be donated to the New England Baptist Hospital.